PIONEER EDITION

By J. J. Kelley and Greta Gilbert

CONTENTS

Paddle to Seattle

Two friends set a difficult goal: to kayak from Alaska to Seattle. Will they succeed?

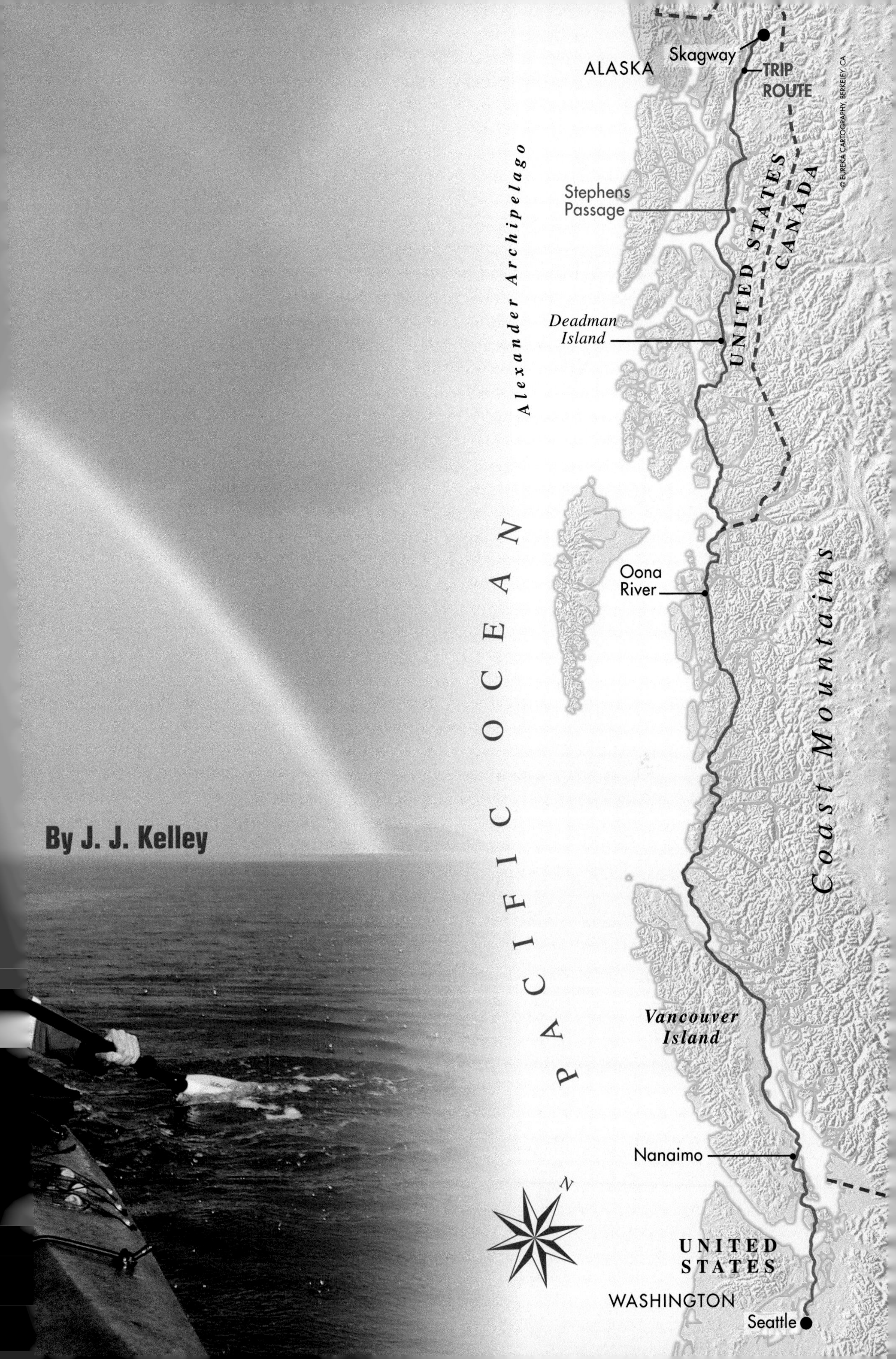
Skagway
ALASKA
TRIP ROUTE
Alexander Archipelago
Stephens Passage
UNITED STATES
CANADA
Deadman Island
PACIFIC OCEAN
Oona River
Coast Mountains
Vancouver Island
Nanaimo
N
UNITED STATES
WASHINGTON
Seattle
© EUREKA CARTOGRAPHY, BERKELEY, CA

By J. J. Kelley

Josh Thomas and I stand on a cold beach in Alaska. We're starting a trip of a lifetime. We climb into wooden sea kayaks. Our goal is to paddle 2,100 kilometers (1,300 miles) to Seattle. It will take us three months, if all goes well.

We spent a year planning the trip. Josh built the kayaks. We practiced paddling often. Paddling in rough water can be dangerous. We must know how to paddle to stay safe.

We gathered gear, too. We needed a tent. We needed sleeping bags. We needed maps. We packed cameras. We also packed a journal. We want to record everything that happens.

Getting Ready

Finally, we picked our route (see map, p. 3). We couldn't paddle in the Pacific Ocean. The water is too rough. Instead, we chose to follow the Inside Passage. It is a kind of water path. It travels along the coast of the Pacific Northwest. It goes between islands and the **mainland**. The islands block strong waves, winds, and **tides**.

The water is calmer in the passage. Storms aren't as bad. The waves reach one meter. That's better than four meters! The calmer water will make our trip safer. Seattle, here we come!

It took Josh two months to build the kayaks. Here, he glues together the deck of a kayak.

A week before our trip, we try out our kayaks. We're at Bear Glacier in Seward, Alaska. The water is icy cold!

Week 1: Leaving Skagway, Alaska

Bam! A wave hits the deck of my kayak. I close my eyes to keep the rain out. Winds howl. I feel like I can't go much farther. What a first day!

It is our second day. There is more rain and wind. It is too dangerous to paddle. We must wait for better weather. We're wet, cold, and tired.

We learn there is less wind in the morning. It's easier to paddle then. Some days, we start at 5 a.m. Yet by the end of the week, we've gone only 113 kilometers (70 miles). Our goal is 168 kilometers (105 miles) a week. At this rate, it'll take us more than four months to get to Seattle! Maybe this trip isn't such a good idea. . . .

On the fourth night, Josh makes camp in Alaska's rain forest. Here, the trees can grow up to 95 meters (312 feet) tall.

Week 2: Stephens Passage, Alaska

A small group of humpback whales circles our kayaks. One comes up for air. It blows mist into the sky. Ugh! The mist smells like fish!

In summer, these whales go to Alaska. Some swim 8,000 kilometers (5,000 miles) just to get here.

One whale swims under me. I feel helpless. It could toss my kayak like a small stick! I knock on the kayak. Will the sound keep the whale away? *Phew!* It works.

Week 4: Deadman Island, Alaska

Surprise! It's raining. That's because we're paddling past a **temperate rain forest**.

Like tropical rain forests, these places are really wet. Moist air blows in from the Pacific Ocean. Mountains trap the air. The air becomes rain. Some temperate rain forests get 510 centimeters (200 inches) of rain a year.

In a kayak, there's no place to hide from rain. My fingers look like raisins. Mold grows in my sleeping bag.

Then, on day twenty-four, a miracle: no rain! We dry out.

Week 6: Oh, Canada!

Wahoo! We just paddled into Canada! Now we're almost halfway to Seattle!

We have our routine down. Wake up. Eat breakfast. Pack. Paddle.

We see many humpback whales on our trip. One like this could flip our kayaks.

The Inside Passage is a narrow path of water that goes past steep mountains in Canada.

© CHRIS CHEADLE/PHOTOLIBRARY

Eat lunch. Paddle. Unpack.
Eat dinner. Sleep.

We paddle about eight hours a day. I daydream as I paddle, stroke after stroke, hour after hour. Each day feels endless.

We need a lot of energy to paddle. So we have to eat a lot. To add calories, we put butter in all our food. I even tried it in my coffee. That wasn't so good.

At night, we set up camp far from the water. The water can rise six meters (twenty feet). We don't want to wake up wet.

The changing tide along the coast leaves behind bright sea stars like these.

© CARR CLIFTON/MINDEN PICTURES

Week 7: Oona River, Canada

Bad news. We stop for the night in a town called Oona River. A man we meet there tells us, "You're late. Winter storms are coming." He tells us to try again next year.

Is he right? Winter may seem far off. Yet we still have a long way to go. We see signs that the season is changing. The sun sets earlier each day. It is getting even rainier. What if we don't make it? I feel sick.

Bad weather keeps us in Oona River for an extra day. The man's words seem to be coming true. We have been wet and tired for two months now. It's hard to keep going. Yet we won't give up.

Week 10: Vancouver Island, Canada

Our difficult trip continues. One day, the wind is very strong. We paddle less than one mile per hour. Another day, the tides help us move quickly. We go fifty-three kilometers (thirty-three miles) in one day. That's farther than ever.

We safely reach Vancouver Island, Canada. There are only 483 kilometers (300 miles) more to go. Soon, we'll paddle back into the United States. Maybe we'll succeed after all!

Week 13: Seattle!

I see Seattle's skyline. I am filled with excitement. We did it! It's early October. We beat the winter weather.

Now the adventure is over. I'm not sure if I'm happy or sad. Josh and I set a goal. We didn't know if we'd succeed. Would it be too far? Would we get hurt? Would we still be friends after such a hard trip? (Yes, we are!)

Now I feel like I can do anything. There's just one thing left to decide. Where will our next adventure take us?

mainland: main, large landmass

temperate rain forest: forest with cool temperatures where it rains at least 152 centimeters (60 inches) a year

tide: regular rise and fall of the ocean's surface about every twelve hours

© JOSH THOMAS

Sunny days like this were unusual. Here I'm paddling along the Inside Passage near Nanaimo, Canada. The waves and wind make cliffs like this one.

We see our first orcas near Vancouver Island. They travel in groups.

ALASKA STOCK IMAGES/NATIONAL GEOGRAPHIC STOCK

Wendy

Booker and the Seven Summits

Join a real-life action hero as she climbs some of the world's tallest mountains.

By Greta Gilbert

Picture a hero in a story. She is strong. She is brave. She is on an adventure. She is climbing one of the tallest mountains on Earth.

Wind roars through her clothing. Her bones ache. Her fingers are freezing. The temperature is minus forty degrees. "Not too bad," she thinks. She climbs on.

Meet Wendy Booker. She is the hero of a real-life story. She has a goal. She wants to climb the tallest mountain on each of Earth's seven continents. Together, these mountains are called the Seven **Summits**.

Wendy Booker plans to climb Mount Everest. It is Earth's tallest mountain.

The Seven Summits

Booker's journey started in Alaska. She wanted to climb Mount McKinley. McKinley is the tallest mountain in North America. She had to try twice. Finally, she made it to the top. Then she wondered, "What next?"

Booker decided to climb all Seven Summits. Soon she headed to Mount Kilimanjaro in Africa.

On Kilimanjaro, Booker saw something new each day. She saw vines like those Tarzan swings on in movies. She saw trees like the ones that Dr. Seuss draws in books.

A year later, Booker climbed Mount Elbrus in Europe. Then she climbed Aconcagua in South America.

Next, she made it to the top of Vinson Massif in Antarctica. Vinson was tough. Booker had to hike through thick snow. She used a special kind of ax to climb on ice. Yet Vinson was her favorite climb so far.

Finally, Booker climbed Mt. Kosciuszko (kah see US koh) in Australia. It was her sixth summit. Just one summit was left.

The Invisible Enemy

A hero in an adventure story usually has an enemy. Booker does, too. It is multiple sclerosis (MS). This is a serious disease.

MS attacks nerve cells in the brain and spinal cord. The nerves cannot do their jobs correctly.

MS can make people dizzy. It can make muscles hard to control. It makes parts of Booker's body totally **numb**. Yet Booker doesn't let that stop her. With her disease, she climbs on.

Help From Friends

Every hero gets discouraged. The students at Donald McKay K-8 School in East Boston cheer Booker on.

Before each climb, the students give Booker a bag of gummy bears. At the summit, Booker eats the gummy bears. Then she calls the kids on a satellite phone.

Booker visits the students often. She tells about her climbs. She shows her **gear**. Each year, she and the students climb a small mountain together. She wants to show how fun climbing can be.

Climb On!

Soon, Booker will need more gummy bears. That's because she plans to climb the tallest summit of all. She is going to climb Mount Everest in Asia. If she succeeds, she will be one of a few women who have climbed all Seven Summits. She will be the first woman with MS to do so.

No matter what happens, Booker will climb on. "I want to inspire others," she says. "I especially want to help young people. They should not see **obstacles** as mountains in their way."

You may not climb mountains. Yet you can still be the hero in your own adventure story. Think about *your* Seven Summits. How will you climb them?

Wendy Booker climbs a wall of ice on Mount Rainier, Washington.

Wordwise

gear: the special tools or clothes you need for an activity

numb: without feeling

obstacle: something that makes it difficult to succeed

summit: the top of a mountain

Design Your Own EXTREME CHALLENGE!

© MICHAEL NEWMAN/PHOTO EDIT

You don't need to travel the world to face an extreme challenge. You can do it in your own neighborhood! Try it. You can do it!

Step 1: Set a challenging goal.
Is there is a nearby hill you want to climb? A bike or walking path you want to explore? Make a goal for yourself that seems a little difficult.

Step 2: Find an adult partner.
Ask an adult you know to join you. Talk about your goal. Decide the safest way to reach it.

© JASON TODD/RUBBERBALL/CORBIS

© PLUSH STUDIOS/BILL REITZEL/BLEND IMAGES/CORBIS

Step 3: Make a plan. Get a map of your neighborhood. With your partner, find your route. Then decide how long it will take to reach your goal. Use the chart below to help you.

How far, and how long?

Distance	Time on Foot	Time by Bike
1 kilometer (about 1/2 mile)	15 minutes	4 minutes
1 1/2 kilometers (about 1 mile)	22 minutes	6 minutes
3 kilometers (about 2 miles)	43 minutes	13 minutes

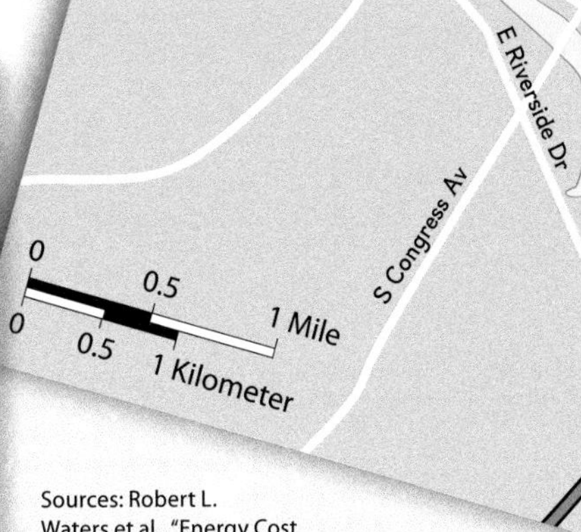

Sources: Robert L. Waters et al., "Energy Cost of Walking in Normal Children and Teenagers," *Developmental Medicine & Child Neurology 25* (1983): 184-188; Diane C. Thompson, "Bike speed measurements in a recreational population: validity of self reported speed," *Injury Prevention 3* (1997): 43-45.

Step 4: Get ready. Gather what you need to complete your challenge. Will you need any special gear? Be sure to bring food, and plenty of water, too. Be prepared!

Step 5: Face your challenge. Go for it! There may be parts of the challenge that are difficult. Ask your partner for help. When you have completed you goal, celebrate. You did it!

Step 6: Share your experience. Tell friends, family, and teachers about your experience. You may want to write about it in a journal or online. Your story can help others reach their own goals!

MEET THE CHALLENGE

Challenge yourself. Answer these questions about how people reach their goals.

1. What goal did Josh Thomas and J. J. Kelley have? How did they reach it?

2. Name two challenges the kayakers faced.

3. Why does Wendy Booker climb mountains? Find sentences that tell the answer.

4. What two questions do you have about the Seven Summits?

5. How are the people in the articles similar? How are they different?